PHENOMENALLY FIT AND Fabulous

A WOMAN'S GUIDE TO BECOMING A MVT - MOST VALUED TREASURE!

DR. DEMETRIA SPRINGFIELD BANKS

All Bible quotations are from the King James Version of the Bible (public domain).

Scripture references that do not have the Bible version noted are the author's paraphrase.

Cover photo by Michael Norman Photography.
Cover design by Its J. Media.

ISBN 978-0-9965947-8-3

Library of Congress Control Number: 2020903076

Copyright © 2020. Demetria Springfield Banks. All rights reserved. No parts of this work may be reproduced or copied in any form or by any means – graphic, electronic, or mechanical; including photocopying, recording, taping or use of any information retrieval system without the express written consent of the author.

PUBLICATIONS BY DR. DEMETRIA SPRINGFIELDBANKS:

*Prayer Pearls: Priceless Inspiration
(Revised Edition)
25 Workplace Survival Tips for the Believer:
Surviving Drama in the Workplace
Every Single One of You: Living Above Single
Life Frustrations
Surviving This Place: 20 Prayers for the Workplace
Healmotions: Unwrapping the Mummy Layers
I Am Somebody That's Who I Am
Between the Watch, the Wait, and God's Work: A
31 Day Journal of Encouragement*

Contents

Dedication	VI
Foreword	VII
Introduction	IX
First Things First...	12
How Do You Define a Phenomenal Woman?	15
MVT Principle One: A Woman of Thanksgiving	17
MVT Principle Two: Values Herself	21
MVT Principle Three: God is Her Source of Validation	26
MVT Principle Four: Perfectly Imperfect	29
MVT Principle Five: Avoids the Comparison Trap	33
MVT Principle Six: A Woman of Determination	37
MVT Principle Seven: An Overcomer	41
MVT Principle Eight: A Warrior not a Worrier	46
MVT Principle Nine: Lives above Her Past	52
MVT Principle Ten: Settling is not in Her DNA	57
MVT Principle Eleven: Her Sister's Keeper	61
MVT Principle Twelve: Her Relationship with God is her top priority	65
MVT Principle Thirteen: Surrendering – Her Key to Success	70
MVT Principle Fourteen: Rids Herself of the Little Foxes	74
MVT Principle Fifteen: A Woman of Unshakable Faith	78
MVT Principle Sixteen: Her Thought Life is in the Right Place	83
MVT Principle Seventeen: She Thinks Big!	86
MVT Principle Eighteen: Her Words are Seasoned Seasoned with Grace	90
MVT Principle Nineteen: Manages Her Home Well	94

MVT Principle Twenty: A Praying Wife	98
MVT Principle Twenty-One: God's Girl (single women)	104
MVT Principle Twenty-Two: A Soul Winner	109
MVT Principle Twenty-Three: A Savvy Business Woman	112
MVT Principle Twenty-Four: Embraces Her Womanhood God's Way	117
MVT Principle Twenty-Five: Not Afraid to Step Out of Her Comfort Zone	122
MVT Principle Twenty-Six: Phenomenally Fit	128
Decrees	131
A Woman of Value	133
A Woman of Purpose	134
A Woman of Confidence	135
A Woman of Faith	136
A God-fearing Wife	137
A Satisfied Single	139
A Successful Woman	140
A Healed Woman	144
Finances	145
An Overcomer	146
Today's Phenomenal Woman Poem	147
Notes	148
Contact Information	149

Dedication

To every woman who has ever struggled with her
self-worth, confidence, identity, past, and or purpose:
May the pages of this devotional be the catalyst
that propels you to greater dimensions
in every area of your life.

Foreword

This devotional, *Phenomenally Fit and Fabulous*, is a by-product of my life coaching masterclass, *The Three V's of Today's Phenomenal Woman*.

After coaching and mentoring many women who struggle with realizing their value and potential in life, I decided to host a free online masterclass that would address today's woman in these areas—her value, her purpose, her past, her future, and her relationship with God.

I discovered that many women have encountered challenging life situations that have negatively impacted the way in which they think and feel about themselves. Some have been victims of abuse—physical, sexual, verbal and mental. Others have been raised in environments that have negatively impacted their self-respect and confidence.

Unable to rise above the negative impact of these things, it is difficult for them to see themselves the way that God sees them—as beautiful, royalty, prosperous, productive, righteous, chosen, and more!

Other women have not experienced unfortunate situations such as these, yet still struggle with knowing their worth, walking in their purpose, and attracting relationships of value.

Each time we offered this masterclass, it met with huge success. Tired of the masks that they have worn day in and day out, many women came to class excited and ready to experience freedom from the weights that prevented them from being the phenomenal woman that God created them to be. They were transparent in sharing their life experiences and ready to open their wounds to receive the healing virtue of God. After each class, testimonies poured about how the class helped them to receive the deliverance, strength, and direction they needed.

I feel great joy as I think about some of the testimonies that we received, confirming God's hand with me to deliver such a class. I knew the time would come when I would write a book on this topic in order to be a blessing to even more women. Well, my sister, that day has come!

Introduction

I spoke at an amazing women's conference in 2018 at a church in my hometown. As I glanced at the program, their theme for the conference really caught my eye. It stated, *"Today's Woman: More than Pumps and Purses."* I thought to myself what a befitting theme for the occasion. To me, it really spoke to the godly woman of today—how she's much more than the clothes she wears or the things she possesses. As I reviewed my notes, I felt God nudging me to deal more specifically with their theme.

Certainly, today's phenomenal woman is much more than pumps and purses. She has it going on, not only on the outside—her demeanor, graceful mannerisms, the way she dresses, and the way she carries herself, but on the inside as well. This woman is classy, intelligent, determined, confident and strong. She is a woman of dignity and meekness. Above all, she is a woman of faith who trusts God completely with her life, relationships, and destiny. Undoubtedly, it is her connection to Him that makes her fit and fabulous in every way.

I could go on and on about her. But before I proceed, let me ask you a few questions:

- Woman, are you ready to become all that God has created you to be?
- Are you ready to rise above the grave clothes of low self-esteem and low self-confidence?

- Are you tired of attracting relationships that de-value you? that steer you away from God?
- Are you ready to walk in your God-ordained purpose?
- Have you decided that the enemy has held you back long enough and today is the day that you are drawing the line against his work in your life?

Then this devotional of empowerment is for you! In this book, I present value keys that will help transform you into this extraordinary woman of purpose. The winning principles that I am going to share have worked for me and countless other women that I have coached. I am where I am and who I am today—an award-wining life coach; an author of seven great selling books; an owner of two businesses and a woman who captured the heart of her Boaz after waiting for forty-four years because I applied these success nuggets to my life.

As with anything, it's the application of information that will lead to transformation. At times the principles will challenge you to forsake your old way of being and embrace the new things God is doing for you and in you. Other times you will reflect because the principles are deep and thought-provoking. You may also cry as you begin to let go of the past—old relationships, friends, acquaintances, and ways of thinking and speaking that have for too long prevented you from being the great woman you were created to be.

Woman of God, get ready to soar! Get ready to walk talk in your purpose. Get ready to reach higher heights in all things concerning you. *You* are a phenomenal woman that's who you are!

First Things First...

> "That if thou shall confess with thy mouth the Lord Jesus, and shalt believe in thine heart that God hath raised him from the dead, thou shalt be saved. For with the heart man believeth unto righteousness; and with the mouth confession is made unto salvation."
> —Romans 10:9-10 (KJV)

As I began with the phenomenal woman online class, so I shall begin this book with this important "housekeeping" business. The principles that I'm going to share with you are based on a woman who has a relationship with the Lord. With that being said, if you are tired of living life your way and would like to become God's daughter, an heiress to His promises, then you can do so today. There is nothing you have to do to earn God's salvation. It is a gift freely given to you (Eph. 2:8).

Pray this prayer with me:

> *Lord Jesus, I am sorry for my sins. You said in Your Word that if I confess my sins, You are faithful and just to forgive me and cleanse me from all unrighteousness (1 John. 1:9).*
>
> *Lord, I receive Your forgiveness and ask that You come into my heart. I believed that Jesus is Your Son and*

> *that You raised Him from the dead. I believe it and confess it.*
>
> *Lord, thank You for coming into my heart. Thank You for saving me. I ask that You empower me to walk in Your will and Your way from this day forward. In Jesus's name, Amen.*

Perhaps you have accepted Jesus as your personal Savior, but have turned from following Him. Now you desire to return to the Lord. The Word of God tells us that the Lord is married to the backslider (Jer. 3:14). If you fall into this category, then pray this prayer with me:

> *Lord, Your Word says You are married to the backslider. I am sorry for my sins. I ask You to forgive me and come into my heart. Cleanse me of all unrighteousness, dear Lord. Strengthen me to stand against the wiles of the enemy that I don't fall prey to his schemes again.*
>
> *Lord, I receive Your forgiveness (1 John 1:9). Thank You for forgiving me. Help me to grow in the grace and knowledge of You (2 Pet. 3:18). In Jesus's name, amen.*

My prayer for you:
Father God in the name of Jesus, I come against every deceptive spirit that tries to convince this woman that her salvation is not real. I bind every

spirit that will try to bring condemnation, guilt or shame for if any man be in Christ he is a new creature. Old things have passed away and behold all things become (2 Cor. 5:17). I pray that You help her to receive Your forgiveness, and also strengthen her to walk in Your marvelous light. In the mighty name of Jesus, Amen.

Now that our houses are in order, let's move forward!

How Do You Define a Phenomenal Woman?

When I asked this question in one of my online classes, here is what a few of the women shared (by permission):

> "Today's phenomenal woman is a woman that strives to go higher in mind, body and spirit. She recognizes her strengths and allows them to propel her higher and keep her balanced; while acknowledging her weaknesses, using them as an opportunity to allow God to build her."   T. Mason

> "Today's phenomenal woman is a woman who believes in who she is and stands up for what she believes. She doesn't let anything or anyone stop her from going after what she wants. She knows that with God on her side, she is going to make it. She doesn't have to compromise. She is a woman called by God."   J. Bailey

> "Today's phenomenal woman can do all things through Christ who strengthens her. She is strong, a leader and, a go getter. She is somebody that's who she is!"   D. Chapman

Awesome definitions aren't they! I tell you there is nothing like a woman who is phenomenal in every sense of the word.

So, as I did in class let me ask you. How do you define a phenomenal woman? Write your definition below. This is important because your definition will serve as a P.O.R.— point of reference as you prayerfully ask God to make, mold and shape you into this woman.

MVT Principle One

A Woman of Thanksgiving

Today's phenomenal woman is most certainly a woman of gratitude and appreciation. Even in a world characterized by ingratitude, she is certain to offer thanksgiving unto God on a daily basis. She thanks Him for what He has done in her life, for what He's doing presently, and for what He is going to do.

She's also careful not to take any of His blessings for granted—thanking Him for the privilege of seeing each new day, being in her right mind, having a home, her family, running water, gas in her automobile, clothes to wear, food to eat, legs to walk with, eyes to see with, the ability to talk, and the list goes on. Even if she lacks some of these things, she is still thankful knowing that He will supply her every need.

Although she has experienced her share of misfortunes in life, rather than complain, she chooses to be thankful because His hand of grace has kept her in the midst of it all. It is indeed her attitude of gratitude that gets her through the difficult places in life. It is her attitude of gratitude that helps her to live above life's stressors.

Rather than focus on what she doesn't have and what's not going her way, she is too busy thanking God for what she does have and what is going for her. Rather than dwelling on what's missing in her life, she dwells on what's not missing—her relationship with Christ. She is mindful of the scripture that instructs her to give God praise in everything—good or bad (1 Thes. 5:14). Moreover, she knows that the secret to moving God to act even more on her behalf lies in an attitude of gratitude, rather than bitterness. The more she thanks Him for what He has done, the more His blessings come her way.

> "Giving thanks always for all things unto God and the Father in the name of our Lord Jesus Christ."
> Ephesians 5:20

Prayer:
Lord in times were many are unthankful, help me to always give You thanks no matter what. I realize that regardless to what I may be going through, You are still worthy of praise. Your goodness to me far outweighs my tests and trials.

During times where I am tempted to complain, help me to refocus and remember that there is someone somewhere who would rather be in my shoes.

Father, keep a praise in my heart and a song on my lips. Strengthen me to bless You at all times. In Jesus's name I pray, amen.

Life Application:

1. Life can give us many reasons to complain. However, today's phenomenal woman chooses to praise God in spite of. List below the many things you have to be thankful for. Refer to this list during times of discouragement and despair.

2. Why is it important to express gratitude to God?

3. If you struggle with an attitude of ingratitude, take a moment to write what thoughts are contributing to your ungratefulness. Then purpose to follow the advice given in 2 Corinthians 10:5 and Philippians 4:8.

Mediation Moment

A woman with an attitude of thanksgiving has a sweet pleasantness about her. Her attitude of thanksgiving is her "beauty secret" that adorns her with joy instead of stress, peace instead of duress, and strength instead of weariness.

MVT Principle Two

Values Herself

Vocabulary.com defines the word *value* as to "regard highly," "to think much of," or "to hold dear." When you value something, it is important to you. You exercise great care in taking care of it, in protecting its value.

The same thing is true when you value someone. You consider them important, worthwhile. You want the best for them. You treat them well, and expect others to do the same. Am I right about it? I can sense you nodding your head in agreement.

Today's phenomenal woman is certainly a woman who values herself. Not because of her physical attributes or her accomplishments. Neither is it because of her prestigious family background, where she works, where she lives, or even where she shops. But her value, her opinion of herself, is based on everything God says about her in His Word. And, let me tell you, His Word speaks well about her.

She has a high opinion of herself; yet she is not conceited. She fully understands that she is a daughter of the King (Ps. 45:13), and that her worth is far more than rubies (Prov. 31:10). Because of this, she doesn't allow anyone to treat her in a manner that doesn't reflect her value. Nor does she accept opportunities that will lessen her value. She knows in God's eyesight she is the "cream of the crop" and refuses to accept less than God's best for her. This woman truly embraces what God says about her and walks in the confidence of the Lord.

God's Word tells her that she is:
- redeemed—bought with the precious blood of the lamb (Eph. 1:7),
- chosen and royal (1 Pet. 2:9),
- the head and not the tail (Deut. 28:13),
- fearfully and wonderfully made (Ps. 139:14),
- made in the image of God (Gen. 1:27),
- industrious (Prov. 31:13),
- strong (Prov. 31:25),
- wise (Prov. 31:26),
- victorious (1 Cor. 15:57),
- purposeful (Jer. 1:5), and
- distinguished (Prov. 31:30).

With such a description by the One who created her, how can she not view herself as an MVT — Most Valued Treasure!

Prayer:
Dear Lord, help me to understand that my value has everything to do with what Your Word says about me and not about my past or personal feelings. As Your Word declares, I am royalty, chosen, fearfully and wonderfully made, and so much more.

When the enemy presents me with lies about myself, help me to resist him knowing that he will flee (James 4:7). Even when he tries to bring up things from my past or mistakes I have made, let me be mindful of Your Word that says if any man be in Christ, he is a new creature. Old things have passed away behold all things are new (2 Cor. 5:17). And, that in You, I am forgiven (Eph. 1:7).

Father, forgive me for the times I have thought of myself in an inferior manner for You have created me in Your very own image. That means, I'm top of the line, special and set aside for a great purpose.

Help me each day to cast down every imagination that negatively impacts the way that I view myself. Help me also to lay aside any negative words I use to describe myself for this is not pleasing in Your sight and is contrary to Your Word.

Father, I thank You that everything You have created, including me, You call very good (Gen. 1:31). Thank You for loving me with an everlasting love. With Your help, I can truly embrace the wonderful identity I have in You. In Jesus's name, amen.

Life Application:

1. How do you value you? Remember that Proverbs 18:21 says that as a man thinketh in his heart so is he.

2. The law of attraction states that "like attract like." Thus, if you're a woman who doesn't value yourself then you're going to attract people who don't _____ _____. On the other hand, if you value yourself, you will attract people who _____ _____.

Why is this so important for you to know?

Which would you like to attract and why?

3. The next time you are tempted to connect with individuals or pursue an opportunity that does not reflect your value, follow these very important steps:
    1. Stop
    2. Think about the consequences
    3. Ask yourself is the individual or opportunity truly worth it in terms of your future, peace, purpose, dignity, and status as a daughter of the King?

Meditation Moment
Remember your value is not determined by your past, mistakes, wrong decisions or anything of that nature. Your value is determined by what God says about you. God knew all about the mistakes, wrong decisions and poor choices you would make. Yet, He still calls you chosen, accepted, righteous and blessed.

Keep in mind that the way you value yourself will affect every area of your life—your decisions, relationships, walk with Christ, career choice, ministry, business, and outlook on life. Thus, embracing God's opinion about you will help you make wise choices in all of these areas.

MTV Principle Three

God is Her Source of Validation

We all desire the approval of others in some form or another. We feel good when others encourage us, give us a compliment, or approve of a decision we make. We also feel a sense of gratification when we are applauded for our accomplishments. After all, we have worked hard and made many sacrifices to accomplish what we have.

However, the problem comes in when we become solely dependent on these things as our measure of worth. What happens when others don't approve of us? Or there is a rift in our relationships? friendships? or marriage? Or what happens when our accomplishments are not recognized, or our careers hit a snag?

While today's phenomenal woman appreciates the compliments and opinions of those she trusts, and is thankful for her achievements in life she seeks her validation solely from God. Her energies are spent making sure she is pleasing to Him.

> "For do I now persuade men, or God? Or do I seek to please men? For if I yet pleased men, I should not be the servant of Christ."
> Galatians 1:10

Prayer:
Father, while we all have a desire to receive validation from family, friends and others we know, help me to not depend on any of these for feelings of significance. Only You are the true source of validation.

O Lord, build me up where I am torn. Help me to become secure in You.

Forgive me for the times I have valued others opinion above Your Word. Forgive me for the times that I have depended on others for validation for with You, I am already significant. In You, my deepest desires are truly fulfilled.

Thank You for helping me. In Jesus's name I pray, amen.

Life Application:

1. Why do some women seek validation from others?

2. Is it wrong to desire validation from others? Why or why not?

3. How can the things such as our accomplishments, possessions, looks, etc. provide us with a false sense of validation?

4. Can a woman love God, but also seek the approval of others? In what way(s?)

5. Who or what do you depend on for validation?

If you struggle with seeking validation from others or your accomplishments, what steps will you take starting today in order to become more God-focused rather than people-focused?

Mediation Moment
When we depend on others for validation, we put ourselves in an endless cycle of always trying to please them. This is not God's will for our lives. He desires for us to focus on pleasing Him. When we please God, everything else falls in place.

MVT Principle Four

Perfectly Imperfect

Today's phenomenal woman recognizes that she is not perfect and is perfectly ok with that. Instead of spending countless hours and days wishing she was more like this and more like that, she accepts her imperfections and knows that while they are a part of her, they do not define her. She is content with leaving the "perfecting business" up to God, relying on Him to perfect all things concerning her (Ps. 138:8).

> "For *all have sinned, and come short of the glory of God.*"
> Romans 3:23

Prayer:
Father, although there are some things I wish I could change about myself, help me to accept the things I cannot change, work on the things that I can change, and leave everything else in Your hand.

Forgive me when I have shown a lack of appreciation for the way that You've created me. Your Word declares that I am Your workmanship created unto good works (Eph. 2:10). To be called Your workmanship is the best compliment I can ever receive.

Lord, thank You for loving me with an unconditional love just as I am. In Jesus's name I pray, amen.

Life Application

1. What does it mean to be "perfect" in God?

2. Write down one woman you really admire. Is she perfect in the sense that she has never made a mistake? That her looks are flawless? That everyone likes her and treats her well?

3. What are the dangers in allowing your mistakes to define you?

4. Don't waste another day being hard on yourself because of the things you don't like about yourself. You've wasted too much time already. It is time for you to rise, my sister, and accept God's wonderful truths about you. Listed below are my "Three Power Challenges " that will help you build positive self-esteem.

   1. **Word Challenge**
      God's Word has lasting transformational power. The more time you spend in it, the more you will begin to see yourself as He sees you.
      So, I challenge you to increase your time in the Word of God. Search the scriptures daily, even several times a day, meditating on those scriptures that speak life to your confidence, future and purpose. As you do this on a continual basis, you will begin to notice positive changes in the way you think and feel about yourself.
   2. **Thought Challenge**
      If you want to stop feeling poorly about yourself, then I challenge you to "flip the script" on your thought life. When negative or demeaning thoughts about you enter your mind, immediately slam the door of entry. Do not hesitate. Do not give them a second thought.
      Instead, think about your strengths and the things that are going well for

you. Think about positive things others have said or noticed about you. Also, think about the beautiful future you envision for yourself. And, more importantly reflect on what God says about you in His Word. Do this again and again.

As you daily practice this important step as well, you will begin to notice the difference in how you think and feel about you.

3. **Talk Challenge**

   Remember the Bible says that death and life are in the power of our tongues (Prov. 18:21). Thus, it goes without saying that if we want to feel better about ourselves, then we should speak better about ourselves. Even if you don't like everything about yourself, begin to speak words of life concerning you, your destiny, value and purpose. If you find yourself drifting back into your old habit of talking because it doesn't seem as if this is helping, continue to press ahead knowing that anything worth having is worth fighting for. Pretty soon positive, life-giving words will begin to replace negative, self-limiting words.

Meditation Moment

If God doesn't require you to be perfect, then why do you?

MVT Principle Five

Avoids the Comparison Trap

Have you ever said to yourself: *I wish I looked more like her? Why can't I be successful like her? I wish my life was more like her life.* Or have you ever scrolled down your Facebook page or any of your social media pages only to see a pretty picture of one of your friends who seems to have it going on in terms of everything causing you say within, "I wish that was me."

Women can be often guilty of comparing themselves to other women in terms of looks, accomplishments, careers, homes, clothes, education levels—you name it. At the root of this type of comparison are distasteful traits of ungratefulness, dissatisfaction, envy and displeasure toward God for seemingly shortchanging you. Certainly, when we marvel at how another woman looks and her accomplishments, while despising how we look and our accomplishments, we are in essence saying to God, "I'm angry with You for the way you created me."

Today's phenomenal woman avoids the "comparison trap" altogether knowing that no good thing will come of it. She understands that if she is to walk in confidence then comparing herself to others will only chip away at her self-worth, causing her to feel that she will never be good enough, smart enough or successful enough.

Or when tempted to compare, she quickly gathers herself together remembering that this is a "no win" situation. Rather than compare herself to other women, she uses God's Word as her measuring rod of truth.

> "For we are his workmanship, created in Christ Jesus unto good works, which God hath before ordained that we should walk in them."
> Ephesians 2:10

Prayer:
Dear Lord, help me to remember that nothing good results when I compare myself to others. This ungodly action can cause me to become unthankful, bitter, and envious—all are which are contrary to Your plan for my life.

If my need for comparison is because of insecurity, I ask You to heal me from any insecurity that I have. If it's jealousy, Lord, please remove it from me because this is not pleasing in Your sight. Yea Lord, whatever the cause may be strengthen me to rise above it.

Lord, I ask You to forgive me for any time I have been dissatisfied with my looks or possessions. I am created in Your image and what a marvelous image that is. And in spite of all the things I do not have, You still are good to me and Your love is great toward me.

Lord, thank You for helping me. In Jesus's name, amen.

Life Application

1. Have you ever compared yourself to another woman? How did it make you feel about yourself, your accomplishments?

2. What are the dangers of comparing yourself to others?

3. What is an inferiority complex and how does it negatively impact what God is doing in your life?

4. What steps are you willing to take to help you avoid the "comparison trap?"

Meditation Moment
In a world where the focus is on who's the best looking, the richest, has the best physique, etc., today's phenomenal woman should ask God to help her find peace with the things she cannot change, bless her with the courage and determination to change the things she can, while thanking Him for what He allows knowing that He is working His will and the do of His good pleasure.

MVT Principle Six

A Woman of Determination

Trials and hardships have come her way, but in spite of it all today's phenomenal woman continues to hold on to God's unchanging hand. She is confident that His grace will sustain her, His blood will cover her, and His hand will provide for her no matter what.

She is truly a woman of determination—determined to press through life's tests; to be the best that she can be both spiritually and naturally; to accomplish her goals, to make a difference, and to live out her God-ordained purpose. Her mind is made up and her eyes are fixed on the prize of being all that God wants her to be (Phil. 3:4).

Yes, she has felt like giving up. At times, she even doubted herself, her purpose and conviction. There were also times she paused along the way because life challenges seemed too difficult to bear. Yet in those moments, she pulled herself together with the help of God, listening to His still quiet voice say, "You've come too far to give up now. Keep pressing forward, My daughter."

Life hardships may have left their scars on her, but the scars testify that she survived because she is a woman of determination.

> "Therefore my beloved brethren, be ye stedfast, unmoveable, always abounding in the work of the Lord inasmuch as ye

know that your labor is not in vain in the Lord."
1 Corinthians 15:58

Prayer:
Lord, help me to be a woman of determination, a woman with a resolve to persevere during the storms of life. Instead of giving up, strengthen me to use life's troubles as stepping-stones to reach my goals and higher heights in You.

O Lord, during times of weariness, refresh my soul. You have promised to give power to the faint and to them that have no might You will increase strength (Isa. 40:29). Yea Lord, in times of distress lead me beside the still waters as You said You would (Ps. 23:2).

With Your help, during troublesome times I will look unto You, the author and finisher of my faith (Heb. 12:2) for strength and direction. You have promised to be a present help in the time of trouble (Ps. 46:1). Thank You for strengthening me. In Jesus's name, I pray, amen.

Life Application

1. Read and meditate on Philippians 3:14 and Galatians 6:9. Write down what you believe God is saying to you through these scriptures.

2. In the Christian race, many start off with great intentions only to end up falling by the wayside because of life's challenges. List three steps you can take that will help you not only start off with great intentions, but also run until you reach your goals in life. When times of testing come, refer to this list as many times as needed until you have strength to press ahead.

3. Write what Philippians 4:13 mean to you. Read it, believe it and declare it again and again in the midst of any struggle you face in life.

Meditation Moment
The word *determination* is defined as "continuing to do something even though it is difficult." Sister I say to you that in spite of life's struggles, keep pressing; keep the faith; keep praying and continue to hold on to God's unchanging hand. Your change will come. You will reap if you faint not.

MVT Principle Seven

An Overcomer

The phenomenal woman of today is an overcomer as well. She is a woman who has stood the test of time and with the help of the Lord prevailed against hardships that have come her way.

Instead of allowing life's difficulties to break her, she has allowed them to shape her into the strong, confident, God-fearing woman that God desires her to be.

She is the woman who others said wouldn't make it and wouldn't amount to much in life. But, because she knew who she was and Whose she was, she defied all odds against her.

She could have decided to give up when life's tests brought her low. She could have turned her back on God, upset with Him that He allowed her to be tried in such a manner. But when pushed to the limit, with tears in her eyes, she held on to God's unchanging hand confident that somehow, some way He would make a way. And, He did.

Attitude is everything when it comes to this woman, and it is her prevailing attitude toward life's troubles that has caused her to be an overcomer. Her attitude consists of these four important things:

1. She's an "anyhow praiser". She responds to life challenges with praise instead of fear despite what she thinks or how she feels. She knows that if God allows it, He will make a way for her to get through it. Indeed, in everything she gives her Father praise (1 Thess. 5:18).

2. She is secure in her relationship with Christ. Because she has spent quality time with the lover of her soul, she knows that to know Him, is to trust Him completely. He has never failed and she is certain that He never will.
3. Her confidence is in God's Word. When facing life obstacles, her confidence is not in her feelings, thoughts, or the well-meaning advice of others. Her confidence is in the Word of God. Since God promises that His Word will not return void, but will accomplish everything He sends it to do (Isa. 55:11), she is certain God's Word concerning her will come to pass. She esteems the Word of God more important for her survival than necessary food (Job 23:12).
4. She is a woman of persistent prayer. She not only talks about prayer, but her life is prayer-centered—talking to the Lord throughout the day, acknowledging Him in all things concerning her life (Prov. 3:5-6).

> "Ye are of God, little children, and have overcome them: because greater is he that is in you, than he that is in the world."
> 1 John 4:4

Prayer:
Dear Lord, Your Word declares that I can do all things through Christ who strengthens me (Philip. 4:13). Your Word also says that I am more than a conqueror (Rom. 8:37) and an overcomer (1 John 4:4).

In times of turmoil and tragedy, help me to stand firm on these important truths. Yea Lord, give me standing power in the midst of life's difficulties. Help me to endure until my change comes.

I believe that there is no problem beyond Your ability to deliver. O Lord, nothing is too hard for thee! Thank You for helping me. In Jesus's name, amen.

Life Application:

1. What does an overcomer mean to you?

    Does your answer describe you?   Why or why not?

2. List one woman in the Bible who in your opinion was an overcomer?

   What was it that made her an overcomer? As you list your answer, ask yourself: Does this description fit me?

3. Trusting God is a vital key in helping us overcome life's difficulties. In your own words define the word *trust*?

   Does your definition describe your attitude toward life's challenges?

4. A close relationship with God provides us with overcoming strength when facing troubles in life.
   On a scale of one to ten, with ten being the highest, rate your relationship with Christ?

If your answer is less than what you desire, what steps will you take to improve your relationship with Him?

5. In your opinion, what is meant by the statement, "God's grace is sufficient for me?"

Meditation Moment:
In this life, we will experience difficulties. Jesus tells us this very fact in John 16:33. However, it is our response to our trials that will determine whether we will prevail or live in defeat.

    Let your response to life's adversities be one of faith and confidence knowing that the Overcomer is on your side to help you prevail every time.

MVT Principle Eight

A Warrior not a Worrier

Instead of worrying about how she's going to make it, this woman knows how she will make it. She is a woman of much prayer, praying about all things—relationships, opportunities, decisions, business ventures, purchases, family, career, you name it.

Without a doubt, praying without ceasing is the essence of her life (1 Thess. 5:17). She understands that if she is going to be victorious, then all of her battles must be fought on her knees rather than pacing the floor.

A lifestyle of prayer makes her a serious threat to the enemy. When he comes against her in any kind of way, she turns to God, confident that when she prays in faith, He will deliver every time (Mark 11:24).

Although anxiety and stress attempt to gain entry in her spirit, they are not a part of her DNA because she knows that a woman who prays is a woman who will stay in perfect peace.

She is a true warrior in prayer, grabbing hold of the altar of God and not letting go until... she receives the very thing she asks for. Her prayers are specific and Word-based confident that when she prays God's Word, His Word won't return void.

She is also strategic in prayer, first appreciating God for who He is and what He has done. Then praying that God's will be done in all things (Matt. 6:10). She also makes sure to ask the Lord for His forgiveness, while she forgives others, understanding that unforgiveness in her heart will prevent her prayers from being answered (Matt. 6:12; Ps. 66:18). She then seals her prayers by praying "in Jesus name" for the Father has made it clear that when she asks in His name He will do what she asks (John 14:13).

She has saved herself from many restless nights and days of worry by being a woman of unceasing prayer. She is truly a warrior, not a worrier.

> "Praying always with all prayer and supplication in the Spirit, and watching there unto with all perseverance and supplication for all saints."
> Ephesians 6:18

Prayer:
Father, help me to be a woman of unceasing prayer; a woman who prays about everything while worrying about nothing. O Lord, help me to spend more time in prayer because when I draw nigh to You, You will draw nigh unto me (James 4:8). And, in Your presence I will have fullness of joy and at Your right hand pleasure forever more (Ps. 16:11).

Lord, I know that it is not Your will for me to worry. You told me in Your Word to be anxious for nothing, while praying about everything (Phil. 4:6). You also said that You came that I might have life and have it more abundantly (John 10:10). That includes living above the stresses and strains of this life.

Father, take out of me any thinking pattern, attitude or behavior that contributes to worry in my life. Yea Lord, deliver me and I shall be delivered. Strengthen me to cast all my care upon You for You care for me (1 Pet. 5:7).

Thank You for helping me. In Jesus's name, amen.

Life Application:

1. Why is a lifestyle of prayer important to today's phenomenal woman?

2. What does praying through mean to you?

Does this description describe you?

3. Why do you think God wants us to pray about everything and worry about nothing?

4. Are you a warrior or a worrier?
   If you're a warrior, what steps are you willing to take to strengthen your prayer life?

   If you're a worrier, how can you become more of a prayer warrior?

5. List three ways you will increase your prayer time. Which one(s) will you make a commitment to do?

6. Write down seven (the number of completion) scriptures that talk about prayer. When life's difficulties threaten to overwhelm you, refer to this list to help bring peace to your soul.

Meditation Moment
You may be going through a trying situation at the moment. I challenge you to pray about it, rather than worry about it. Pray until... you feel a release in your soul.

Remember God's Word says that the effectual fervent prayer of the righteous man <u>availeth</u> much (James 5:16). Simply put, your praying is not in vain.

MVT Principle Nine

Lives Above Her Past

You may think that you don't deserve anything good to happen to you because of what has happened in your past. Or feel that because of your past, there is no way you could ever accomplish something great in your life. But let me tell you this one thing, woman of God, God can and will make something beautiful out of your life. There is not a mistake that you can make that the blood of Jesus won't wash its stain away. With God as the head of your life you are a prime candidate to receive the goodness of the Lord in the land of the living.

God has a way of taking battered, broken and shattered lives and transforming them into something beautiful and amazing. He has a way of turning the hurt from our past into glorious testimonies.

Remember Rahab? She was a prostitute; yet God used her as a part of His divine plan to give His people victory (Josh. 2:1-25). She is also listed in the genealogy of Jesus (Matt. 1:5). How about Esther? She was an orphan. Yet, God blessed her to marry a wealthy king and used her to save His people from extermination (the book of Esther). Then there was Ruth. She was a poor, young widow who God blessed to marry the most eligible bachelor in town that happened to be very rich, I might add (the book of Ruth).

God really has a way of using the most unlikely candidate to accomplish great things for Him when that individual submits their life to Him. Today's phenomenal woman knows this and lives by it. Her past is just that—her past. She has decided that it will not become her future.

> "...forgetting those things which are behind, and reaching forth unto those things which are before."
> Philippians 3:13

Prayer:
Dear Lord, help me to leave my past in the past and move forward to the glorious future that You have for me. Regardless to things that have happened, Your Word declares that Your thoughts and intentions toward me are of peace, not of evil to give me an expected end (Jer. 29:11). Let me be mindful of that truth.

When the enemy or others try to remind me of my past, help me to remember that in You I am no longer condemned (Rom. 8:1); that I am forgiven and redeemed (Eph. 1:7)); that old things have passed away and all things are become new (2 Cor. 5:17); and that my sins have been washed by the precious blood of Jesus (Isa. 1:18).

Lord, I thank You for the new life I have in You. I may not be everything I desire to be, but I am thankful that I'm not what I used to be. In Jesus's name I pray, amen.

Life Application:

1. Great women such as Maya Angelou, Joyce Meyers, and Oprah Winfrey all suffered traumatic experiences while growing up. Rather than allow past tragedies to define them, they rose above them and went on to accomplish great things. Why? Because they refuse to allow their past to dictate their future.

   In what ways have you allowed your past to hinder you from moving forward?

   What will you do to rise above these things?

2. What does the Word of God say about your past?

3. List five (the number of God's grace) scriptures on God's power to heal. Meditate on these scriptures daily. The more you embrace them as truth, the more God's healing virtue will become a reality in your life.

Meditation Moment
You are still here which means that your past did not destroy you. It also means that you still have the opportunity to take advantage of the great plans that God has for you.

Woman of God, God's power to birth greatness out of you is at your disposal. Tap into it today by crying out to Him. He has promised to answer when you call regardless to what has happened (Ps. 55:10).

I challenge you today to gird the loins of your mind and grab a hold to these two important truths:

1. You <u>can</u> let go of your past for you can do all things through Christ who strengthens you (Phil. 4:13). It will take hard work and commitment, but remember anything worth having is worth working for, and
2. Your past does <u>not</u> have to determine your future. Let me repeat this. Your past does not have to determine your future. With God on your side, you can beat any and all odds against you (Rom. 8:31). He is the God that makes all things new (Rev. 21:5).

MVT Principle Ten

Settling is not in her DNA

Many times we are guilty of cheating ourselves out of God's best by having a "settling" mentality. We say things like "I've applied for position after position and yet I've gotten nowhere. It's not meant for me to get a better job." Or "I've been dealing with this condition so long that I don't believe it's God's will to heal me." Sometimes single women say, "Rather than be alone, I'll just settle for this man," all while knowing that that man is not God's will for them.

While we know that God's will for our lives supersedes our thoughts and feelings on any given day and at any time, we must never accept less than what His will is for us because of how we feel or what we see. Today's phenomenal woman understands this very well. In the midst of the temptation to settle in any area of her life, she makes the decision to wait on God. Her choice is based on three things:

1. The price her Savior paid by sacrificing His life for her is too high a cost for her to settle.
2. The consequences of settling for something not meant for her is too costly in terms of the negative impact it will have on her life.
3. She is fully persuaded that what God has promised her, He shall perform regardless to the obstacles,

opposition or timetable involved (Rom. 4:21).

"If a man die, shall he live again? all the days of my appointed time will I wait, till my change come."
Job 14:14

Prayer:
Dear Lord, when I am tempted to settle for less than Your best, strengthen me to hold on to Your unchanging hand. Help me to wait on Your good and perfect gifts for me.

I believe that all of the promises in You are yea and amen, and that they will come to pass (2 Cor. 1:20). I also believe that no good thing will You uphold from me as I walk uprightly before You (Ps. 84:11).

In times of weariness, You have promised to refresh me. You are indeed the saving strength of Your anointed (Ps. 20:6). I also believe that You are able to keep me from falling and to present me spotless before the presence of Your glory with exceeding joy (Jude 1:24). Thank You for helping me. In Jesus's name I pray, amen.

Life Application:

1. Why would a woman settle for less than God's best?

2. What are the dangers in settling for anything or anyone that is not God's will for you?

3. Does settling for less indicate a lack of trust in God to know what's best for you? Why or why not?

4. Why is it important for God's leading lady to know her worth when it comes to her choices in life?

Meditation Moment:
My dear, realizing that you are God's creation and the apple of His eye (Gen. 1:31; Ps.17:8) are important nuggets to keep in mind when making any decision concerning you. If God thinks enough of you not to give you second best, shouldn't you think enough of yourself not to settle for less?

MVT Principle Eleven

Her Sister's Keeper

In today's world of the "me movement," where the focus is on "I," "me," and "my," today's phenomenal woman is not only concerned about her own well-being, but she is also concerned about the well-being of her sister. Not to receive a pat on the back or any type of recognition, but she is genuinely concerned about her sister's welfare.

It doesn't matter if it is a sister by birth or someone she knows, works with, attends church with, or whatever the case may be. She respects her and loves her with an unconditional love.

When her sister hurts, she hurts. When she rejoices, she also rejoices. When her sister needs someone to lean on, she is there. She's her sister's cheerleader, confidante, and even her vote of confidence when she's hard on herself.

She's also her sister's accountability partner, applauding her when she makes progress and praying for her when she falls short.

Today's phenomenal woman also doesn't judge her sister. Yet she will gently and wisely confront her when she's in the wrong.

When she hasn't seen her in a while or notices that her sister hasn't been around, she calls, texts or goes to visit her to make sure all is well. Without hesitation, she goes the extra mile when her sister is in any type of need.

Instead of joining in when others are speaking against her sister, she quickly ends that pointless conversation by saying, "Let's pray for her."

Her sister's secrets are safe with her even when they have a disagreement. What's shared in confidence remains in confidence. She wants nothing less than God's best for her sister. She is her sister's keeper.

> "... but in lowliness of mind let each esteem others better than himself."
> Philippians 2:3

Prayer:
Lord, bless me to be my sister's keeper in every sense of the word. There are those You have placed in my life for such a purpose as this. Help me to be wise in my relationship with them, steering them in the direction that You would have them to go. Let genuine love and pure intentions reign in my heart toward them. In Jesus's name, I pray, amen.

Life Application:

1. What is your definition of a sister's keeper?

2. Are there any women in your life that you are a sister's keeper to?   If so, in what way(s)?

3. Are there any women in your life that you feel God nudging you to serve as a sister's keeper? If so, who are they and have you reached out to them?

If not, pray and ask the Lord to lead you in this area.

4. How can you become an even better sister's keeper?

Are you willing to commit to what you wrote?

Meditation Moment
Have you checked on your sister lately?

MVT Principle Twelve

A Relationship with God is Her Top Priority

When it comes to relationships, her relationship with God is at the top of her list. She loves Him. She adores Him. She longs to spend time with Him every day.

When she wakes up, He is the first person she talks to. Throughout the day, her mind often thinks about Him. He is the apple of her eye and wind beneath her wings. He is her everything.

Because her relationship with the Lord is her top priority, today's phenomenal woman is on guard for anything and anyone that threatens to negatively impact her relationship with Him. She understands that without Him, she would be nothing. But with Him, she has it going on.

No man has ever treated her royally the way He does. No man has ever given her the world while expecting nothing in return like He has. That's why she invests so much in their relationship. There is no doubt in her mind that He truly loves her and is concerned about her total well-being.

She doesn't have to worry about losing out when it comes to her goals, career, business, ministry, or any relationship. It is because of her relationship with Him that all these things are in order.

"That I may know him, and the power of his resurrection, and the fellowship

of his sufferings, being made conformable unto his death."
Philippians 3:10

———————

Prayer:
Father, it is a delight to be Your daughter. Thank You for saving me.

Lord, I long to know You more and to draw closer to You each day. Yea Lord, as the deer panteth for the water brook my soul longs after You (Ps. 42:1).

Fill me with the knowledge of Your will in all spiritual understanding. Let my desire be those things that are above (Col. 3:2) which are sure to strengthen my relationship with You.

Lord, help me to stay on guard for anything that will steer me away from You no matter how innocent it may appear. Also, give me the strength to part from anything and anyone that interferes with our relationship. Continue to lead me in the way that You want me to go.

Thank You, Father, for ordering my steps in Your Word. Thank You for helping me to achieve an intimate relationship with You. In Jesus's name, I pray, amen.

Life Application:

1. The Bible tells us to desire the sincere milk of the Word that we may grow by (1 Pet. 2:2). One way we can strengthen our relationship with the Lord is by spending time with Him in His Word—finding out how He thinks, how He feels, what grieves Him, what brings Him joy, etc.

   Decide on a time that you will set aside each day to read the Word of God. Write it below. Then sign the commitment. This is an agreement between you and God. So, don't take it lightly. Of course, other things can come up that may alter the time and days you list below. If so, don't stop. Simply adjust your days and time.

   The purpose of this exercise is to help strengthen your relationship with God. The more time you spend with Him on a daily basis, the stronger your relationship will be.

   Perhaps you already have a set time of daily mediation. In that case, decide on how you will increase your time in the Word.
   We can talk all day about having a stronger relationship with God, but until our words turn into action, we will be as sounding brass and tinkling cymbal.

Day(s) & Time(s):

Name: _____ **Date:**_____

2. It's also imperative that we spend time in prayer with God. This is another important key to having a strong relationship with Him.

   Prayer is simply talking to God. No fancy words or even correct grammar has to be used. Simply talk to Him out of your heart. Keep in mind that prayer also involves two-way communication. So, once you finished praying wait to hear what God has to say to you.

   As you spend time in prayer on this week and weeks to come, use the chart below to write what He says to you.

   Monday:

   Tuesday:

   Wednesday:

Thursday:

Friday:

Saturday:

Sunday:

Meditation Moment:
Many times, the emptiness we feel in life is actually a longing in our souls created by God for more of Him. We discover, like the woman at the well (John 4), that Christ is only one who can completely satisfy our thirsty souls. Life truly becomes more meaningful and fulfilling as we invest time in building our relationship with the Lord.

You will also find that things that used to bother you will not work your nerves as much. Not to say that everything will be perfect, but because of your intimate relationship with Him little trivial things that use to agitate you will begin to lose their effect on you.

MVT Principle Thirteen

Surrendering – Her Key for Success

Some of the seasoned mothers in our church would often say that to surrender to God means to give up your right to be right. That in Christ, it is no longer about what we want, but about God's will for our lives.

When I think of the term surrender, I think about someone giving up their rights to a greater authority. For example, when an individual is placed under arrest he or she is told to surrender, to give up to the policeman in charge. This is also the case when a battle is fought. I remember seeing in some western movies the losing side lifting up their arms, surrendering to the winning side.

Today's phenomenal woman surrenders her entire life to her Lord. She prays daily, "*Not my will, Father. Thy will be done.*" She knows that if she is to be victorious and experience success in any area of her life, then she must surrender her wishes, desires, goals, dreams, and plans to the Lord trusting Him to know what's best for her.

On days where she struggles with her will verses His will because what she wants seems to be just what she needs, she calls on the Lord for help for He is her high priest who can be touched with the feelings of her infirmities (Heb. 4:15). The more she surrenders to Him, the more she wants to surrender because His intentions toward her are pure and to bless her beyond her imagination (1 Cor. 2:9).

"I am crucified with Christ: nevertheless, I live; yet not I, but Christ liveth in me: and the life, which I now live in the flesh I live by the faith of the Son of God, who loved me, and gave himself for me."
Galatians 2:20

Prayer:
Dear Lord, have Your way in my life. I surrender everything to You – my thoughts, words, marriage, family, relationships, fears, insecurities, decisions, health, weaknesses, strengths, career, goals, ministry, business—everything concerning me. You know what is best for me.

Help me to see that surrendering is not a sign of weakness, but of strength and total trust in You. It is the road that leads to Your perfect will being done in my life. It is the key to good success.

Even in times when I don't understand Your leading, strengthen me to follow Your way. Lord, thank You for helping me. In Jesus's name I pray, amen.

Life Application:

1. In your opinion, what does it mean to surrender to God?

2. If you have not fully embraced your definition, what steps will you take beginning now?

3. What does the statement, *God knows what's best of for me,* mean to you?

Refer to your answer in times where you struggle with His will verses your own will.

Meditation Moment:
If you're looking for success in any area of your life, try surrendering it to the Lord. You'll be amazed at the rewards that will follow!

MVT Principle Fourteen

Rids Herself of the Little Foxes

One of my favorite prayers in the Bible is found in Psalm 51:10 where King David prays,

> "Create in me, O God, a clean heart and renew a right spirit within me."

Although David was described as a man after God's own heart (1 Sam. 13:14), every decision he made did not honor God. He made the poor choice of committing adultery with Uriah's wife (2 Sam. 2:11). However, once he was confronted with his actions, David expressed great sorrow. He didn't try to blame anyone else or make excuses for himself. He came clean before God and prayed the prayer above.

While the sin he committed is what some may label as a "big sin," today's phenomenal woman recognizes that *any* sin, no matter how big or small is something that will defile her, as well as grieve her Father. Thus, she watches out for "little foxes" such as jealousy, envy, malice, bitterness, strife, competition, a bad attitude, a combative disposition, a revengeful spirit, an unruly tongue, and evil thinking. These things, she understands, can do just as much damage as what we call "big sins."

Consequently, a prayer of spiritual cleansing is a part of her daily routine even praying it several times throughout the day if need be. God has invested too much in her and she has made too many sacrifices to miss the mark because of "little foxes" being in her life.

> "Take us the foxes, the little foxes, that spoil the vines: for our vines have tender grapes."
> Song of Solomon 2:15

Prayer:
Dear Lord, it is not my sister or my brother, but it's me standing in the need of prayer. I don't want my living to be in vain.

Please take out of me what is not pleasing in Your sight. Whether it's a sin of omission or commission, forgive me Lord. If it's a "secret" fault, a bad thought, or even distasteful words, forgive me.

As King David prayed, purge me with hyssop and I shall be clean. Wash me and I shall be as white as snow. My desire is to please You in all things. Thank You, Lord, for cleansing me. In Jesus's name, amen.

Life Application:

1. "Little foxes" as mentioned in this principle are such things as a negative thought, hurtful words, a bad attitude, etc. What other "little foxes" can you add to this list?

2. Why is it important for us to repent of the little foxes in our lives? After all, it's a little fox. Surely no harm can be done by it. Right?

3. "Pop-Up Prayer." I challenge you to pray what I call "pop-up prayers."

   A "pop-up prayer" is simply a prayer of repentance prayed immediately when we know that we are doing, thinking, saying, or reacting to something in a manner that is not pleasing to God.

This exercise will help you become more aware of the things we label as "little sins" and don't really feel a need to ask God's for forgiveness, but should. Praying pop-up prayers will also help keep our vessels pure and ready for the Master's use.

Meditation Moment:
All sin is sin. It doesn't matter if we categorize it as a big sin or a little sin. It still grieves and disappoints God. It's still something we need to confess and ask for forgiveness.

MVT Principle Fifteen

A Woman of Unshakable Faith

Today's phenomenal woman is also a woman whose faith doesn't shake even in the most trying circumstances. Her response is "No matter what. I believe God." She knows it's her job to trust God and it's His job to provide for her. And He does so continually.

It is her unshakable faith that has brought her through many rough valleys in life. That opened closed doors on her behalf. That made ways for her when there was no way. That turned 'no' answers to 'yes' answers. That brought her consolation when she needed it most. That held her family together through the toughest of times. That provided her with the healing she needed for her mind body, and soul.

Even when discouragement and weariness try to take over her soul, it is her unshakable faith that tells her to hold on because God's help is on the way. She is indeed a remarkable woman of faith trusting God completely.

What is it that keeps her faith strong in the midst of trying circumstances?

1. She immerses herself in God's Word. She knows that faith comes by hearing and hearing by the Word of God (Rom. 10:17). Thus, if she wants stronger faith then the Word of God is the place to be on a frequent basis.

2. She prays without ceasing (1 Thess. 5:17). Praying is the fuel that keeps her faith alive and strong in the midst of heartaches and heartbreaks.
3. She's a continual worshipper, giving God praise not only when things are going in her favor, but also when they are not.
4. She's a woman full of gratitude rather than of complaints. Her attitude of gratitude during life's troubles testifies to her unwavering faith in God.

"Being fully persuaded that what He promised, He was able to perform."
Romans 4:21

_____

Prayer:
Lord, help me to be a woman that believes Your promises no matter what. Regardless to what I see or how I feel, let me not waiver in my faith. You said that a double-minded individual is

unstable in all his ways and will not receive anything from You (James 1:6-8).

When my faith becomes weak, help mine unbelief (Mark 9:24). Help me to see that Your power to deliver is greater than my trials.

Lord, if there are any strongholds in my life hindering my faith from becoming strong reveal them to me that I may repent. If there are any thought patterns or attitudes that contribute to my lack of faith, strengthen me to overcome them.

Lord, I believe that with Your help my faith is growing stronger each day. In Jesus's name, amen.

Life Application:

1. What is the definition of faith according to the Bible?

   What is your definition?

In times of difficulties reflect on this definition to help strengthen your faith.

2. What causes us to doubt God?

   How can you overcome these obstacles?

3. How do our "what if" statements hinder us from standing firm in our faith?

4. Fear is the opposite of faith. How have you allowed fear—fear of the unknown, fear of what may happened, fear of what has happened, etc. negatively impact your faith?

5. Fervent prayer, daily doses of God's Word, and putting the Word of God into action can help strengthen our faith. What else can you add to this list?

Meditation Moment:
Although we are tempted during trying times to focus more on our problems than God's ability to deliver, remember that there is not a test that you and I can face that is beyond God's power to help us. Nothing is too hard for the God that we serve.

MVT Principle Sixteen

Her Thought Life is in the Right Place

An online article by *Charisma Magazine* entitled, *Power of the Tongue: Words can bring death or life,* states that we think 70,000 thoughts daily on the average. Can you imagine that! I don't know about you, but this statistic really causes me to take a second look at my thought life.

Then the Bible states in Proverbs 23:7 that *as a man thinketh in his heart, so is he*. This scripture lets us know that our thoughts are very powerful. They are powerful enough to create and shape our reality!

Really think about that for a couple of moments. Let it sink in. Absorb it with all your being. If we truly believe God's Word is undeniable truth, then we as God's daughters should strive daily to control the type of thoughts we allow to enter in our mind. Thoughts of negativity, doubt, discouragement and fear should not be on our guest list of entry.

Today's phenomenal woman lives by this scripture principle faithfully. Every day she makes a conscious effort to think on those thoughts that are faith-full and that will shape and mold her life into what she desires it to be, while discarding negative, hope-dashing thoughts. She has found that when her thought life is in the right place, her actions, reactions, attitude and her words are influenced in a most beneficial way.

"Finally, brethren, whatsoever things are true, whatsoever things are honest, whatsoever things are just, whatsoever things are pure, whatsoever things are lovely, whatsoever things are of good report; if there be any virtue, and if there any praise, think on these things."
Philippians 4:16

Prayer:
Dear Lord, help me to cast down every thought that is contrary to Your Word. I know that my thoughts are powerful. They influence all that I say and do. And if I am to live victoriously, I must obey the Word when it comes to my thoughts.

It is Your Word that will renew my mind. It is Your Word that will help keep my thought life in order.

Lord, help me to think on those things that are true, honest, just, pure, lovely, and of good report (Phil. 4:8). These thoughts will help me walk in righteousness and truth. They will also help me to keep my mind stayed on You.

Lord, I realize that discarding old thinking habits can be challenging, but with Your help I can do it. Thank You for helping me. In Jesus name I pray, amen.

Life Application:

1. In what ways has negative thinking impacted your life? even on today?

2. How can you break this pattern?

Meditation Moment:
Take time to meditate on Proverbs 23:7. If that is a true statement, and we know that it is, wouldn't it behoove us to fill our minds with God's Word rather than Satan's lies? Or our own limited thinking?

    Remember, no one can force you to think negatively. That choice is yours. What is your choice?

MVT Principle Seventeen

She Thinks BIG!

When it comes to her life, this woman of grace thinks big. She knows that nothing is impossible for the God she serves. From her dreams, to her goals, family, career, finances and purpose, she dares to believe God for the supernatural in these areas.

Limited thinking is not a part of her being because she knows that limited thinking creates limited living, opposite of the abundant life Christ promises (John 10:10). Neither is her thought life consumed with thoughts such as, "What if," "I don't think," or "I'm afraid." These types of thoughts, she reminds herself, will only keep her in an endless cycle of wishing, wanting and waiting.

She is confident that her God is the God of miracles, signs and wonders. That's exactly what she believes Him for. That's exactly what her thought life centers on.

> "Now unto him that is able to do exceeding abundantly above all that we can ask or think according to the power that worketh in us."
> Ephesians 3:20

Prayer:
Lord, You are the God of miracles, signs and wonders. Absolutely nothing is too hard for You. You will do exactly what Your Word says You will do.

Help me to take the limits off of You in all things concerning me. Let my thought life reflect the spiritual truth of who You are and what You can and will do.

Help me cast down any thought preventing me from believing in Your miraculous power. In Jesus's name, amen.

Life Application:

1. What causes a person to doubt God?

2. How has limited thinking affected your life?

3. Below are three tips to help you overcome small thinking.
    1. Ask God to help you discard "what if" scenarios and to help you trust Him more. Remember "what if" thoughts will always keep you wishing and never possessing.
    2. Often times we prevent God performing the miraculous in our lives by trying to control every detail concerning us. We know to give everything to the Lord; however, in our human frailty we still busy ourselves with trying to solve our own problems. What a big mess this sometimes makes!
    Instead of trying to control everything about your life, allow God to control everything concerning you. This gives Him the space to do what He does best—perform the miraculous.
    3. Let go of how you think things should be done. How many times have we said to ourselves, "Well, I thought...?" Ladies, I know sometimes we just can't help ourselves. However, thinking this way will only hinder God's wonder-working power from flowing in your life.
    Remember, God's ways are not our ways and His thoughts are not our thoughts. He is infinite. We are finite. He is all-knowing, we are not. He has an unlimited number of ways of working things out on our behalf. As such, God

can never be reduced to working the way we think He should.

Meditation Moment:
When we think big, we honor God because it shows we are taking Him at His Word. On the other hand, when we think small, it shows that we don't really have the faith we claim we do in God's ability to do the impossible.

MVT Principle Eighteen

Her Words are Seasoned with Grace

Along with keeping her thought life in check, today's phenomenal woman also strives to keep her words in check. She knows that words of anger, gossip and slander have the potential to destroy lives and homes. As such, she exercises care when talking to others, asking God to give her what to say and how to say it.

Rather than using her words to tear down, she uses them to edify and encourage, often pushing others to be the best that they can be even when they don't believe in themselves.

Those who know her enjoy conversing with her for God has given her the tongue of the learned to know how to speak to them who are weary. She is the "go to" person when others need a word of wisdom or hope.

She also speaks words of life to her husband and children—speaking favorably over their life, purpose, identity and destiny. She knows the power of a life-speaking wife and mother.

When speaking the truth, it's never to hurt or based on her emotions. **Emotional speaking, she is convinced, will tear down far more than it builds.**

Even when talking to her Father, her words are a delight to His ears, full of adoration and reverential respect.

Because her words are seasoned with grace, she brings glory to her Father.

"Let no corrupt communication proceed out of your mouth, but that which is good to the use of edifying, that it may minister grace unto the hearers."
Ephesians 4:29

Prayer:
Dear Lord, help me to be a woman whose words are seasoned with grace that I may minister grace to hearers and bring glory to You. Let my words be a blessing to all—my spouse, children, co-workers, friends, and whoever I may come in contact with.

When I am tempted to criticize or use words of judgement, let me be mindful of what You would say and how You would say it. When I am tempted to respond out of anger or abruptly, help me to speak a soft answer knowing that a soft answer turns away wrath, but grievous words stir up anger (Prov. 15:10).

Lord, You have provided me with the greatest example of humility for when You were falsely accused, lied on, and eventually hung on the cross, instead of expressing words of anger and bitterness, You spoke words of compassion asking Your Father to forgive those who mistreated You.

Thank You for such a great example. Empower me to be more like You each day. In Jesus's name, Amen.

Life Application:

1. It has often been said that women are "emotional creatures." That we often speak based on our emotions and feelings. Ladies, we know this to be true.
   Why is this both good and bad?

2. Why is it important for today's phenomenal woman words to be seasoned with grace?

3. List three scriptures that deal with the power of our words. Use them as "friendly reminders

when tempted to use your words in a negative manner.

Meditation Moment:
It's easy for us to speak unpleasant words when we are hurt, upset or even stressed out. However, God requires more of us as His daughters. Our guiding thought when speaking at any time should be, "What would Jesus say?"

MVT Principle Nineteen

Manages Her Home Well

Managing her home well is at the top of today's phenomenal woman's list. Make no doubt about it. Her career, ministry and goals are important, but even more important is the family that God has blessed her with.

She strives to be the wise woman who builds her home in every way (Prov. 14:1). Her daily checklist includes ensuring that her home is well kept, her husband and children are fed, clothes are washed, homework done, and all other family needs are taken care of.

In addition, family time is a must with her. Whether it's praying, eating or playing together. She makes certain not to allow any of her extracurricular activities to crowd her family time or family responsibilities. She asks God to help her be a woman of balance.

Because she recognizes her innate ability to be the "fragrance" of her house, she models love, joy, forgiveness, honesty and trust—traits that are certain to bring a peaceful and delightful aroma in her home.

Rather than resent the fact that she's a mother and wife because she feels it hinders her ability to do things she enjoys, she embraces her roles while thanking God for the strength to carry them out in a manner that glorifies Him. She is truly a builder of her family in every way.

"To be discreet, chaste, keepers at home, good,
obedient to their own husbands,
that the word of God be not blasphemed."
Titus 2:5

Prayer:
Lord, help me to be a good keeper of my home which will be a blessing to both my husband and children. Give me the strength to perform my tasks each day to the best of my ability.

Help me to prioritize my responsibilities so that nothing goes lacking.

Lord, remove from me any feelings of ingratitude, unforgiveness, and resentment. Open my eyes to see the many blessings of being a mother and wife.

Strengthen me to model peace, love and understanding before my family. Yea Lord, let my light shine before them that they may see my good works which will bring glory to Your name.

On days when I feel drained and overwhelmed with my family responsibilities, renew my strength. On days when I am frustrated or upset because things are not going in the way I desire for my family, Lord, renew my focus and help me to cast my cares upon You. I know that You are concerned about me.

Lord, thank You for helping me to be a woman who manages her household well. In Jesus's name I pray, amen.

Life Application:

1. Do you feel that it is a blessing to be a wife?   A mother?   Why or why not?

2. If you don't feel this is a blessing, pray this prayer with me:

    Lord, in spite of how I feel I thank You for blessing me to be a mother/wife. Your Word says that every good and perfect gift comes from You. Thank You for my gifts of being a godly wife and mother.
    Father, forgive me for the times I have not felt this way. I know this is not pleasing in Your sight. Rather than focus on the things that will cause me to resent my

roles, help me to focus on the blessings that each of these roles bring.

I admit that managing a household can be challenging at times, but with Your help I can succeed. You will be a present help for me in times like these. Thank You, Lord, for helping me. In Jesus's name, amen.

3. List five (the number of God's grace) scriptures that can help you when you feel overwhelmed as a mother/wife.

Mediation Moment
Ask God each day to help you be the wife and mother He wants you to be.

MVT Principle Twenty

A Praying Wife

Since she desires the best for her marriage, she knows that prayer is the key that will help make that happen.

One of her constant prayers is "Not my will Lord, but thine will be done." Sure it's not an easy prayer for her to pray at all times, yet her determination to please God outweighs her desire for anything else.

She is the first to admit that she doesn't have the roadmap on what it means to be a good wife. So she humbly submits to the Lord, asking Him for godly wisdom on building her marriage, pleasing her husband, and taking care of her home.

As a praying wife, many of her prayers are not only for her husband—his well-being, needs, finances, fatherhood, temptations, protection, health, guidance, career, responsibilities and such, but even more are daily prayers for herself as his wife. She prays fervently for her mind-set, temperament, emotions, reactions, words, bad habits, and character asking God to remove from her anything that will hinder her marriage from being its best.

Her desire to be a wife of love and peace far outweigh her desire to be right, even when she is right. She knows the power of a praying wife.

"Who can find a virtuous woman? For her price is far above rubies. The heart of her husband doth safely trust in her, so that he shall have no need of spoil."
Proverbs 31:10-11

Prayer:
Lord, strengthen me to be more of a praying wife. Prayer, not fussing or complaining, is the key that will unlock many doors of blessings for my marriage.

Rather than try to influence my husband with nagging, arguments, or harsh words, help me instead to pray for him, asking You to lead, guide and help him wherever he needs help.

Take out of me every wrong attitude, feeling, and thought that will hinder my marriage from being its best. Yea Lord, help me to be more understanding, loving, and considerate.

When I feel I have every right to point the finger or point out his flaws, help me, Lord, not to do so. This will only put unnecessary strain in my marriage. You've instructed me to pray not point my finger.

Lord, help me also to resist the need to "prove my points" or to respond with "I told you so," even when I am right. Bringing glory to You will do far more for my marriage than me being right.

Moreover, help me to realize that I can't control him, his responses, actions, words or thoughts. *The best prayer I can pray in this regard is to pray, "Lord, change me."*

Lord, I desire to be the best wife that I can. With Your help I will be victorious against shortcomings that hinder me. With Your help, I will be a blessing to my marriage rather than a hindrance.

Lord, thank You for helping me to build a marriage of respect, openness, trust, and love. In Jesus's name I pray, amen.

Life Application:

1. Do you have the ability to change your spouse? _____ If your answer is no, then why do you think many wives try to change their husbands?

What happens when we try to change our spouses?

While, I believe God has given women the ability to influence their husbands, none of us have the power to change them. And as God-fearing wives, it is our responsibility to use our influence in godly ways.

2. Wives, many of us acknowledge our shortcomings, but some are guilty of using the excuse of "This is just the way I am."
Are you sometimes guilty of this? Why is this not a good thing to do?

Ask yourself: *Would Christ want me to remain as I am?*

3. If the way we are hinders us from being a good wife and negatively impacts our marriage, is this truly how we want to remain?

If your answer is no, what steps will you take today to change? Only write down what you will actually do. Remember, it takes action to bring forth change.

4. When you pray for your spouse, do you pray for his shortcomings? strengths? Finances? his role as a father and husband? his love for you? his job? God's purpose for his life? things about him that irritate you?

Or are you so frustrated with him in these areas that you fail to pray? Ask yourself: *Has my frustration with my spouse changed anything in our marriage?*

What other areas can you add to this list?

5. What are the biblical characteristics of a godly wife?

Let your list be the mark that you strive toward.

Mediation Moment

Regardless to how you think you should respond or react in situations in your marriage or how others tell you how you should respond, always rely on the Bible as your sole source of guidance. Its strategies and instructions will bless you with the type of marriage of your dreams.

MVT Principle Twenty-One

God's Girl (single women)

The designer label worn by today's phenomenal single woman is the label of being God's girl. She's so in love with Him, often blushing when others remark on how much she resembles him.

She delights in getting His opinions on everything because she knows He truly loves her and wants what's best for her.

She has daily dates with Him, confident that He will never stand her up. During their dates, they talk about His plans for her life. She asks questions. He listens and then gives her the best advice she could ever receive to help her navigate through the journey of life. She also listens attentively as He speaks to her, absorbing His every instruction to her.

God's girl is on guard for anyone and anything that will interfere with her relationship with Him. Too much is at stake, she reasons.

Even on those days where the pains of loneliness seem too much for her to bear, she has learned to draw closer to Him for in His presence is the comfort that she needs.

When she falls short in her walk with Him, she promptly repents determined that nothing will separate her from His love.

He is truly the apple of her eye, the pep in her step, and the smile on her face. Her closeness with Him is the envy of many.

Instead of resenting her singleness, she embraces it, trusting Him to know what's best for her.

> "The unmarried woman careth for things of the Lord, that she may be holy both in body and in spirit."
> 1 Corinthians 7:34

Prayer:
Dear Lord, You said in everything to give thanks for this is Your will concerning me (1 Thess. 5:18).

Lord, I thank You for it is Your will for me to be single at this time in my life. What a marvelous way to be. Your Word has so many wonderful things to say about me as a single woman. I am blessed and highly favored by You.

Lord, help me to embrace my singleness and enjoy life to the fullest. Open my eyes to see all of the wonderful opportunities available to me. Grant me the needed motivation to take advantage of those opportunities.

In times of despair, let me run to You, the Prince of Peace. In You is peace for my soul.

When feelings of self-pity try to overtake me, let me experience Your unspeakable joy. During times where I struggle with feelings of rejection, help me to remember that I am already accepted and loved by You.

Strengthen me, O Lord, to walk in the spirit and I shall not fulfil the lust of the flesh (Gal. 5:16). You have already given me everything I need to live upright before You (1 Pet. 1:3).

Instead of spending countless days and nights wishing I were married, Father, let me find contentment in You. Put Your joy deep down in my soul. Elevate my thinking above my circumstances. I know You will supply my every need.

Lord, thank You for strengthening me. Thank You for loving me with a love that has no strings attached; a love that wants the very best for me. In Jesus's name, I pray, amen.

Life Application:

1. Keep a journal. When I was single, journaling was a great way for me to release my emotions when I felt overwhelmed as a Christian single. I felt free to express my deepest thoughts and most intimate longings with the One I knew who would not judge me; who would give me the help I needed most.
2. List three reasons why it's beneficial to wait on God when it comes to a relationship as oppose to running ahead of Him. Refer to this list when waiting seems unbearable.

3. Write five scriptures that will give comfort to you during trying times of being a single Christian woman. Reflect on these scriptures as often as needed when you feel overwhelmed.

4. Ladies, our most vulnerable times are what I call "empty times" – when we have too much time on our hands, particularly as single women. Consider these things:
   1. Become involved with a hobby that you know that you will enjoy. I love to write. So, I would often write encouraging "sermonettes" and then give them to others who were going through difficult times. Encouraging others will in turn encourage us.
   2. Use this time to go back to school and further your education or learn skills that will help you obtain a new career. Sure it will cost money, but remember

God will give you the desires of your heart when you delight in Him (Ps. 37:4). With God on your side, the sky is the limit to what you can have!
3. If you have dreamed of owning your own business, now is a great time to do research and talk to others who have been successful in the type of business you desire. Don't allow your "what if's," and "I don't think's," stop you from becoming a successful business owner. Remember with God you can do all things.
4. Become a volunteer. This will help fill your idle time with something rewarding. In particular, try to volunteer in areas related to your career choice. This will strengthen your resumé as you look for employment or promotion.
5. Become involved with an auxiliary or department at church. Remember, God has called us to be much more than a pew member. There's a gift, a calling, a talent that He has placed in you that will surely be a blessing to the body of Christ.

Meditation Moment:
If God doesn't pity you as a Christian single, then why should you? Why should you allow others too?

Principle Twenty-Two

A Soul Winner

Today's phenomenal woman is more concerned with turning hearts, than heads knowing that her Savior is soon to return. She doesn't want to be caught with her work undone.

She is busy in the highways and hedges compelling others to give their lives to One who has never let her down (Luke 14:23).

No, she's not timid when it comes to sharing the good news of Christ. Like the woman at the well, she boldly invites others to "come see a man" who will change their life forever; who will not look down on them because of mistakes they have made; who will look beyond their faults and see their need to be whole again.

Even more, the life she lives testifies to others of God's saving grace and power to redeem. She is a soul-winner for her Lord.

> "The fruit of the righteous is a tree of life;
> and he who winneth soul is wise."
> Proverbs 11:30

Prayer:
Dear Lord, put a stirring down in my soul to be about Your business of soul winning. I know that You are soon to return. Help me to take advantage of every opportunity presented me to tell others of Your saving grace.

Yea Lord, fill me with Your Holy Spirit as You did Your disciples on the day of Pentecost (Acts 2:2) so that I can with power and authority witness for You. In Jesus's name, amen.

Life Application:

1. Why do you think some Christians do not witness as they should?

   Do you feel this way?

2. Why is it important to be a soul winner?

3. Write down three scriptures regarding soul winning. Make sure to include scriptures on women who witnessed for Christ.

Meditation Moment
Have you witnessed to anyone today?

Principle Twenty-Three

A Savvy Business Woman

When it comes to business, this woman has her head on straight. With the help of the Lord, she's busy making moves, aware that faith without works is dead (James 2:26).

She's always at the drawing board asking God to bless the work of her hands. Rather than lean on connections she has, she leans completely on the Lord trusting Him to connect her with the right connections, at the right time and right place. She recognizes that with God on her side, good success in business is inevitable.

All her decisions concerning her business are first presented to Him, for the heart of a woman may plan her way, but God establishes her steps (Prov. 16:9). Rather than trust her feelings or "gut instinct," regardless to how big or small the decision is she's always asks "Lord, what shall I do?"

In her business dealings, she is professional, strong, and assertive; yet gentle and longsuffering, allowing her decisions, communications and attitude to reflect Christ.

She owns her business but is careful not to allow the business to own her. Like the Proverbs 31 woman she doesn't neglect her household duties for the sake of a good business deal. She makes sure to ask God to help her to achieve the proper balance in these areas.

> "And whatsoever ye do, do it heartily, as to the Lord, and not unto men."
> Colossians 3:23

Prayer:
Dear Lord, bless the work of my hands. I desire my business to be all that You want it to be. Order my steps and decisions in Your Word (Ps. 119:133). I know I can trust You to lead me in the way that You want me to go.

Bless me with the right connections that will help advance my business in the way You desire. Also, bless my business with faithful clients and customers so that it will grow.

Help me to employ those who are the right fit, who will help me execute the business vision You have given me. Let my dealings with them and my customers be fair and honest.

Lord, bless me with favor and good success. Open doors that no man can shut. Shut doors that You have not opened.

Thank You for supplying me with everything I need for a successful business. In Jesus's name, I pray, amen.

Life Application:

1. Why is it important to put God first as a business owner?

2. As a business owner, is it more important for you to rely on your "gut feeling" or to trust God? Why?

3. Write down the vision you believe God has given you for your business. If any of it is not clear, ask God for clarity.

4. What action steps have you taken toward accomplishing this vision? Remember, faith without works is dead (James 2:14).

5. Ask God to align you with a mentor that will help you to become the businesswoman He wants you to be.

Meditation Moment:
As business owners, it is so tempting when we get a good idea to dive in quickly. But as Christian business owners, we know that good success comes from God. As such every decision concerning our business should be brought to Him.

Certainly, with God as the CEO of your company expect nothing but good success! Hard times will come and sometimes you will be at a standstill. And sometimes you will feel as if you have failed altogether. But in those times realize that because you have acknowledged God in every way, He is going to guide you safely through.

If you have not asked God for His direction, repent and then ask Him for guidance.

Principle Twenty-Four

Embraces Her Womanhood God's Way

In today's society, the "ideal woman" is attractive, aggressive, self-sufficient, outspoken, voluptuous, strong-willed, and career driven. She is the woman who is in control of everything and controlled by nothing or no one.

This is in contrast to God's lady who is God-lead, God-sufficient, God-focused, and God-driven. Whereas society's ideal woman is self-centered and operates from a sense of entitlement, God's woman is God-centered and knows without God on her side, she would be nothing.

Recognizing that man's thoughts are not God's thoughts, today's phenomenal woman embraces her womanhood God's way. She uses her femininity in ways pleasing to God—yielding her rights to the Lord, serving others rather than herself; boasts of her dependence on God rather than her own independence, while serving her husband and children faithfully.

Rather than using her femininity in deceptive, manipulative and seductive ways, she uses it to model humility, strength, godliness and love—a big turn on to any godly man.

Instead of drawing attention to herself because she's that independent woman who doesn't need a man, she draws attention to herself because she's a woman who needs the Man.

She is not headstrong. She is heart strong, having a heart longing to please her Father in every way. She is strong-willed but in a godly manner—uncompromising about the things of God.

Submission is not a curse word with her. It is the principle that aligns her with God's will for her life, bringing her closer to Him.

Rather than view the way God created her in contempt, she accepts it knowing that God did not create her inferior. How could He since she is made in God's own image!

> "...In the day that God created man,
> in the likeness of God made he him;
> Male and female created he them;
> and blessed them..."
> (Genesis 5:1-2)

Prayer:
Lord, thank You for the beautiful gift of womanhood. Let me embrace this gift with thanksgiving rather than contempt. I know that this may put me out of step with mainstream society, but I would rather be more in step with Your will for my life.

Lord, although the enemy has done a number on many women today, causing them to feel that Your values for womanhood are old fashioned, weak, out-of-step with life, and inferior, Your Word is still right and true. It is Your values that will empower me to become the great woman You designed me to be. It is Your values that will give me the greatest sense of satisfaction and fulfillment that I will ever experience in life.

Thank You, Lord, for Your design for me. In Jesus's name I pray, amen.

Life Application:

1. Why do you think Satan, the father of lies, wants women to focus on becoming society's ideal woman than God's ideal woman?

2. Do you think that you will be victorious and satisfied in life when you follow Satan's ideal of womanhood as oppose to God's ideal of womanhood? Why or why not?

3. Search the scriptures. What is God's idea of womanhood?

Use this list as your prayer guide when asking God to mold and make you into the woman He desires you to be.

Meditation Moment:
Even some Christian women view God's ideal of womanhood as something weak, helpless, boring, and unaccomplished. The word submission is a word to be avoided at all costs to them.

They are under the misunderstanding that they will be most fulfilled when they strive to be today's phenomenal woman society's way. However, woman of God, this cannot be further from the truth. Striving to be society's ideal woman will leave you feeling empty, and in some cases meaningless.

Why do you think some women who have accomplished great things in life, are financially well-off, and belong to some of society's elite clubs (both

Christian and non-Christian) still struggle with unfulfillment? From the outside looking in, they appear to have the "ideal" life. However, behind closed doors many feel unfulfilled.

In addition, trying to cope with the void that they feel they drain the life out of their husbands, children, family and friends, trying to get from them what only God can give.

Woman of God, becoming God's phenomenal woman will bring you more satisfaction and fulfillment you can imagine. You will gain so much more when You lose yourself in Him.

Not to say that it will be easy, and perhaps at times even you will think you're weak, too soft, boring and out of step with being a real woman. Trying it may be, but it will be totally worth it! Anything that God designs is totally worth it. After all, He's the master engineer!

Principle Twenty-Five

Not Afraid to Step Out of Her Comfort Zone

The online Oxford Learner's Dictionary defines a *comfort zone* as "a place or situation in which you feel safe or comfortable, especially when you choose to stay in this situation instead of trying to work harder or achieve more." It's a place where no risks are involved; where one is comfortable—comfortable with status quo; comfortable with mediocrity.

Comfort zones are something we all have. Whether doing things the way we've always done them, holding on to a particular way of thinking or being as a way of protection, or making safe decisions because we fear the unknown, we all have comfort zones.

Today's phenomenal woman understands that God not only wants her to survive in life, but also thrive in life. As such, she is not afraid to take a leap of faith outside of her comfort zone in order to possess her promise land.

For her, greatness lies on the other side of comfort. Whether that's being great as a woman, wife, mother, business woman or woman of the Lord, she is willing to take risks in order to live her life to the fullest and reach her full potential.

She is wise enough to acknowledge God even in her risk-taking, confident that where He guides He will provide.

In moments where fear and uncertainty try to prevent her from making a move, she calls on her

Lord remembering that He has not given her a spirit of fear.

> "Have I not commanded you? Be strong and courageous. Do not be frightened, and do not be dismayed, for the Lord your God is with you wherever you go."
> Joshua 1:9

Prayer:
Lord, help me to lay aside excuses, feelings of inadequacy and fear when You are leading me to step out of my comfort zone. Like Abraham, help me to step out in faith trusting You to guide me every step of the way. I don't want to be guilty of living with regrets or missing great opportunities that You have in store for me.

I know that nothing good or productive results from fear. Fear can prevent me from obtaining my dreams, and even cause me to override Your leading.

My desire is to rise above the graveclothes of mediocrity so that I can be all that You want me to be and accomplish everything You have designed for You.

I am confident that with Your help I will not be afraid to launch out into the deep and accomplish great things in my life. With Your help, I will realize my fullest potential. In Jesus's name, amen.

Life Application:

1. What are some excuses we make when it comes to stepping out of our comfort zone?

Remember an excuse regardless to how "legitimate" it may be, can cause us to miss out on God's blessings, and great opportunities of growth.

2. What are the dangers of remaining in your comfort zone?

3. How have you allowed your comfort zone to prevent you from pursuing opportunities—naturally or spiritually?

4. As I stated earlier, most of us have comfort zones. For many of us, they have been a part of our lives for years. Yet if we are to realize our fullest potential, then it is necessary we take needed steps to help us get out of that counterproductive state.

   Here are a few simple steps to help you:
   1. Ladies, first be honest with yourself. Many times, we fail to take action because we are afraid of stepping into the unknown. I think it's our human

nature to draw back when travelling an unfamiliar path. However, it's okay to admit our fears to the Lord in prayer. Remember He has promised to help us in our time of need. So, if you're afraid, simply admit it. You don't need an excuse with God.

2. Next, ask yourself, *"What is it that I'm really afraid of?"* Usually if we search ourselves, we can pinpoint the reason we don't move out of our comfort zones. I've have searched myself many times and have always been able to pinpoint the source of my fear.
3. Once you determine the root cause of your fear, ask God to deliver you from it. If God is able to raise the dead (and we know that He is), certainly He is able to move you out of your comfort zone.
4. Also, think about the consequences of staying where you are – how it will impact your goals, dreams, future, etc. Is that what you really want? This should be enough to stir you to action!
5. Also think about the benefits of stepping out of your comfort zone. Here again, your answer should be enough to get you moving.
6. Finally, write down a prayer asking God to help you to lay aside the weights of fear, mediocrity, discouragement and any other weight that's preventing you from moving forward. It can be the same prayer I listed earlier or write one of your own.

Make sure to ask God to help you lay aside all excuses, including "legitimate" ones. Then, pray this prayer in faith daily. Remember, the effectual fervent prayer of a righteous man will avail much (James 5:16).

In addition, our faith will grow and fears diminish as we spend time with God.

Meditation Moment:
Woman of God, you've dwelt where you are for too long—so long that you have stopped dreaming, your creativity has stifled, and you have accepted status quo as the way of life.

My sister, it is time for you to rise and conquer the land! What is it that you have always dreamed of doing? that God has given you to pursue? Isn't it worth pursuing? Imagine how you will feel when you have accomplished your dreams.

If that's what you truly desire, shouldn't that be motivation enough for you to step forward today?

Principle Twenty-Six
Phenomenally Fit

Not only is today's phenomenal woman concerned about her spiritual well-being, but she also is concerned with being fit physically.

Thus, her weekly and in many cases daily routine, includes eating foods that are healthy, getting proper exercise, and taking time out for times of meditation. She knows that she can accomplish more for God with a healthy body and a clear mind.

Moreover, as God's girl she doesn't want to be "out of shape" in any kind of way. So, her exercise routine also includes monitoring what she allows inside her temple—the type of music she listens to, the type of movies she watches, and the type of literature that she reads. She doesn't want to give place to the enemy in any kind of way.

Getting proper rest is also a must for her. A worn out body and an exhausted mind means one moody woman who no one wants to be around!

"What? Know ye not that your body is the temple of the Holy Ghost which is in you, which ye have of God, and ye are not your own?"
1 Corinthian 6:19

Prayer:
Lord, help me to take care of my temple in every way. I desire to be strong, healthy, and in good shape so that I can serve You to the best of my ability.

Grant me the wisdom to develop a wholesome diet and the will power to stick to it. Yea Lord, increase my appetite for the foods that will promote good health, while decreasing my desire for foods that are detrimental to my health.

Lord, if I lack motivation to exercise, help me, O Lord. Increase my motivation and determination to exercise daily. Consistent exercise will be a blessing to my body, mind and soul.

Lord, forgive me for times I have overate and indulged in activities that negatively impacted my temple. I know that my body is the temple of the Holy Ghost and I do not want to do anything that will grieve Him.

With Your help, I will be phenomenally fit in every way. Thank You for helping me. In Jesus's name I pray, amen.

Meditation Moment
It is God's desire that we prosper and be in good health, even as our souls prosper (3 John 1:2).

So, rise up woman of God and take control over the care of your temple. Don't try to do too much at one time. Each small step will push you closer to your goals. Here's a list for you:

1. Daily walks. These walks can do wonders for you, not to mention they will help clear your mind.
2. Taking the stairs instead of the elevator can provide you with exercise as well.
3. In addition, if you work at a desk like I do, getting up to stretch or even walk periodically also helps.
4. Take advantage of commercial breaks. The next time your favorite movie takes a commercial break, take a break from the couch and do some steppin'! Come on ladies—1, 2, 3, 4! You got it!
5. If possible, get a fitness trainer to help you with your goals. An exercise partner can also be beneficial to you. The motivation that each of these provide can do a lot to keep you going.
6. Try eating healthy foods. You will find that many healthy foods are some of the best tasting foods out on the food market! The only thing that is missing with many of them are the hundreds of calories that we don't need!

Remember ladies, doing something is better than nothing. Also, we lose out when we stop trying. So, if you fail to follow through, don't park there. Get up and keep pushing.

Decrees

Job 22:28 says, "Thou shalt also decree a thing, and it shall be established unto thee: and the light shall shine up thy ways." This mean we can speak with authority and it shall come to pass.

The word *decree* is defined as "an official order issued by a legal authority." That means when an order is issued all parties must abide by its terms.

Let me share an example. I currently work in a court system. When a judge (the legal authority) makes a ruling, the parties have no further say in the case, and must abide by his court order.

In the same way in the spiritual realm, God's Word is the "court order" that carries the authority of God. So, when we decree God's Word of healing for our bodies, for example, this means that anything aimed against God's healing has no authority to prevent it. That decree will come to pass.

Because God's Word is His will for our lives, our decrees are most effective and transformational when His Word is the basis for our decrees as oppose to our own thoughts, wishes, or plans.

On every page hereafter, is a decree that you can use to speak life over your life. Woman of God, if we're looking for change in any area of our lives, it will undoubtedly begin when we exercise the authority God has given us in His Word to decree His will for our lives. It's time exercise the authority given you.

I challenge you to speak one or all of the decrees if they apply to your situation on a daily basis, even several times a day. You can also write your own. Then make a commitment to speak them regardless to what your mood is, how upsetting your day was, or what you think.

Trust me. Some days you won't feel like speaking them, especially in moments of anger or when something occurs that will shake your faith in God. However, rise above your feelings. You can do it. Stay committed to the task. Remember the just shall live by faith, not feelings.

Speak it. Believe it. Stand on it. Then watch how your life begins to change in the direction of your decrees!

A Woman of Value

I DECREE that I am a woman of significant value because God's Word describes me as royal, chosen, peculiar, and holy.
I DECREE I am beautifully, fearfully and wonderfully made because I am made in the image of God.
I DECREE that regardless to my age, shape or size I am a woman of grace, style and dignity.
I DECREE that because I embrace what God's Word says about me, I have no need to compare myself to others.
I DECREE that I have something valuable that God can use.
I DECREE that I will speak words of value about myself on a regular basis regardless to how I feel or what I think because death and life lie in the power of what I speak.
I DECREE that because I value myself I treat myself with care, love, and respect.
I DECREE that I will let go of any negative thought or feeling that I have about myself because this is not pleasing to God and negatively impacts my self-esteem.
I DECREE that I will no longer allow my past or the opinions of others affect how I value myself. I am not my past. I am not who others say I am. I am who God says I am.
I DECREE that because I am God's girl I settle for nothing less than God's best in any area of my life.
I DECREE that I am God's designer's original destined for greatness.

A Woman of Purpose

I DECREE that I am a woman of great purpose, shaped and molded in the image of God.
I DECREE that I have clear direction of who I am and where I am going because God leads me daily.
I DECREE that every day God is making my purpose clearer to me.
I DECREE that daily I make strides toward fulfilling my God-ordained purpose because God's help is with me.
I DECREE that God is aligning me with individuals who will help me to fulfill my purpose because He is ordering my steps in His Word.
I DECREE that God shall supply me with whatever I need in order to accomplish my life's purpose.
I DECREE that nothing and no one will hinder God's purpose for my life because I abide in Him.
I DECREE that daily God gives me the courage, determination and motivation I need to walk in my purpose.

A Woman of Confidence

I DECREE that I a woman of confidence—confident in who God made me and in my skills and abilities.

I DECREE that I walk in confidence because I follow God's directions for my life.

I DECREE that God has equipped me with the ability to make wise, competent and sound decisions regarding every aspect of my life because I acknowledge Him in every way concerning me.

I DECREE that I do not allow my mistakes to define me. They are learning opportunities that will help me grow.

I DECREE that I am destined for victory not defeat because in Christ I am victorious.

I DECREE that with God on my side I will step confidently into my future.

I DECREE that with God's help I face my fears with confidence.

I DECREE that my thought life and conversation reflect godly confidence.

I DECREE that I am a confident woman who knows how to turn down opportunities that are not God's will for me or will over obligate me.

I DECREE that I do not struggle with an inferiority complex because in God I am good enough in all things.

I DECREE that my confidence is growing every day as I abide in Christ.

A Woman of Faith

I DECREE that I am a woman of unshakable faith in a faithful God.

I DECREE that because my faith is God-based even in challenging situations it stands the test of time.

I DECREE that I will speak the Word of God in faith to every crisis situation in my life in obedience to my Father.

I DECREE that each time I pray I do so in faith, nothing doubting.

I DECREE that fear will not weaken my faith for God has not given me the spirit of fear but love, power and a sound mind.

I DECREE that during times where my faith is challenged, the Spirit of God will quicken me and empower me to hold on to my faith.

I DECREE that my emotions will not dictate my faith. My emotions are under the authority of God's Word.

I DECREE that my faith will result in miracles, deliverances and breakthroughs occurring in my life, and in the lives of all who are connected to me.

I DECREE that daily I study God's Word which will continue to increase my faith.

A God-fearing Wife

I DECREE that I am the wise wife of Proverbs 31, who builds her home, takes care of her family, who honors and respects her husband and whose heart her husband trusts.

I DECREE that I am a wife of peace and not confusion; strength and not weakness; love and not hate.

I DECREE that I am a wife of submission because this pleases God.

I DECREE that I am a wife who daily covers her husband in prayer.

I DECREE that because God is helping me no root of bitterness, resentment, anger or strife will overtake me. Neither will they have place in my marriage.

I DECREE that old habits, old ways of thinking and speaking that will prevent my marriage from being its best will not have a foothold over me.

I DECREE that because I am God's girl tendencies of nagging, moodiness and complaining have no control over me.

I DECREE that my reactions during difficult times in my marriage will be to pray and not fuss, complain or nag because greater is He that is in me than he that is in the world.

I DECREE that the Spirit of God guides me in my decisions concerning my marriage.

I DECREE that God gives me successful ideas to maintain the love, spontaneity and passion in my marriage.

I DECREE that my marriage is one of prayer and trust.

I DECREE that no weapon formed against my marriage will not prosper.

I DECREE that because the Lord is our shepherd, we will not lack.

I DECREE that my spouse and I love each other unconditionally.

I DECREE that my marriage is characterized by fidelity as designed by God.

I DECREE that God is healing my marriage of hurt, anger and unforgiveness.

I DECREE that my husband is becoming the man God created him to be.

I DECREE that every day my marriage is becoming what God wants it to be.

A Satisfied Single

I DECREE that I am single and satisfied living pleasing unto the Lord.

I DECREE that my desire is to cleave to God and not to the things of this world.

I DECREE God is providing me with everything I need.

I DECREE that rather than resent my singleness I embrace it joyfully as God's will for me at this time.

I DECREE that my desire for a mate will not override God's will for me.

I DECREE that every day God is providing me with the strength I need to wait on His timing.

I DECREE that while I wait on God He is strengthening me to think on those things that will edify, while casting down those thoughts that will bring my spirits down.

I DECREE that in times of loneliness and despair, I will stand strong and call upon the name of my Lord. He has promised to hear when I call.

I DECREE that distasteful traits of bitterness, resentment, and anger toward my single state have no place in me.

I DECREE that God is giving me great ideas on how to enjoy my life to the fullest as a Christian single.

I DECREE that every day I will experience the joy of God while I wait on Him.

I DECREE that because I am God's girl tendencies of nagging, moodiness and complaining have no control over me.

I DECREE that every day I am becoming the woman that God wants me to be.

A Successful Woman

I DECREE good success in every area of my life.
I DECREE that all of my goals—spiritually, professionally, and relationally will be achieved because God is my helper.
I DECREE that any hindrances to my goals have been brought to naught by the power of God.

Spiritually:
I DECREE that daily I am growing in grace and in the knowledge of my Lord and Savior, Jesus Christ.
I DECREE that daily God gives me the motivation and inspiration to read His Word.
I DECREE that my times of prayer are effective and powerful.
I DECREE that my prayer life is increasing.
I DECREE that my discernment is increasing and I can readily sense the needs of others.
I DECREE that God is filling me with the knowledge of His will in all wisdom and spiritual understanding.
I DECREE that daily the Spirit of God empowers me to walk in a manner worthy of my Savior.
I DECREE that power of God is healing me everywhere I have been torn so that I can be an effective witness for the Lord.
I DECREE that I can hear the voice of God clearly.
I DECREE that my level of faith and obedience has shifted to higher levels.
I DECREE that every power within and around me preventing me from maturing in God will be destroyed by the power of God.

I **DECREE** that God is strengthening me to be a mighty warrior in Him.

Professionally (career, business or ministry):
I **DECREE** that my career/business/ministry is thriving and successful in every way because I have surrendered it to the Lord.

I **DECREE** that God is giving me successful money-making ideas and tips to push my business/ministry to the next level.

I **DECREE** that God is opening enormous doors relative to my career/ business/ministry.

I **DECREE** that my career/business/ministry decisions are wise and productive because God is ordering my steps.

I **DECREE** that promotion and advancement are mine because God promised to give me the desires of my heart as I delight in Him.

I **DECREE** that my career/business/ministry is a tremendous blessing to others.

I **DECREE** that the vision God has given me for my business/ministry is quickly coming into fruition.

I **DECREE** that because I acknowledge God, I attract successful, righteous opportunities.

I **DECREE** that even in difficult times God is causing my business/career/ministry to be successful and grow.

I **DECREE** that God is providing me with an answer to every question I have regarding my business/ministry operations.

I **DECREE** that no weapon formed again my career/business/ministry will prosper.

I DECREE that God endows me with wisdom every day to complete my job assignments successfully and timely.
I DECREE every day peace exist on my job, and in my business/ministry.
I DECREE that God's favor is causing me to advance on the job/in business/in ministry.
I DECREE that God is giving me the motivation and courage needed to make wise moves concerning my career/business/ministry.
I DECREE that all my needs are supplied relative to my career/business/ministry.

Relationally:
I DECREE that because I acknowledge God first, I attract relationships that are God-ordained.
I DECREE that any relationship in my life that is not of God will cease immediately.
I DECREE that where pain and hurt exist in my relationships that God is replacing it with love, joy, patience and understanding.
I DECREE that God is giving me the wisdom to handle misunderstandings and conflict His way.
I DECREE that God is giving me the strength to walk in forgiveness and love in my relationships for this pleases Him.
I DECREE that God is giving me the strength to rise above retaliation because He will fight my battles.
I DECREE that my relationships are healed of confusion, strife and division.
I DECREE that broken family relationships are being restored.

I DECREE that my relationships at work are fruitful, productive and peaceful. Where there is back-biting and division, God is replacing it with love and understanding.

I DECREE that no weapon formed against any God-ordained relationship in my life will prosper.

I DECREE that my relationships are blessed and God-centered.

I DECREE that my relationship with God is growing stronger every day.

A Healed Woman

I DECREE that with Jesus' stripes my body is healed and made whole.
I DECREE that any abnormality, sickness, disease or infection will not reign over my body.
I DECREE every unhealthy cell is being removed by the power of God.
I DECREE every unhealthy bone is being healed by the power of God.
I DECREE that all of my body systems shall function as they were created to function.
I DECREE that any blocked artery or vein in my body will be opened by the power of God.
I DECREE that any infection or inflammation will dissolve by the power of God.
I DECREE that generational diseases are not a part of my body.
I DECREE that God is providing me with the motivation I need to properly care for my body.
I DECREE that God is helping me to eat healthy which will promote good health.
I DECREE that I will be in good health and prosper even as my soul prospers that I may serve God to the best of my ability.
I DECREE that any mental, emotional healing and spiritual wound I have is being healed completely by the power of God.

Finances

I DECREE that God will supply all of my financial needs according to His riches in glory by Christ Jesus.

I DECREE that because the Lord is my shepherd I shall not want.

I DECREE that because I honor God in my tithes and offerings, I shall not lack.

I DECREE that as I seek the kingdom of God first and it's righteousness, all things, including financial freedom will be added unto me.

I DECREE that God is restoring my finances because He promises to restore all the years destroyed by the locust, cankerworm and palmerworm.

I DECREE that God is giving me successful solutions to any financial problems I face.

I DECREE God helps me to make wise financial decisions.

I DECREE that God is giving me the wisdom to develop a budget and the will power to stick to it.

I DECREE that because God is removing from me over-spending habits, impulsive spending, selfishness, greediness, the need to compete with others, and the sense of entitlement, I will not be overwhelmed by debt.

I DECREE that because I am God's daughter, I am a lender and not a borrower.

An Overcomer

I DECREE that I can do all things through Christ which strengthens me.

I DECREE that I am victorious over any challenge in my life because God is my helper.

I DECREE that because the Holy Spirit dwells on the inside of me I am empowered to overcome the spirit of jealousy, envy, manipulation, bad moods, swinging temperaments—any little fox that prevents me from being what God wants me to be.

I DECREE that I have victory over my past.

I DECREE that no weapon formed against me in any way shall prosper.

I DECREE that because I wear the whole armor of God I shall overcome.

I DECREE every hindrance and obstacle impeding my progress is destroyed.

I DECREE that nothing will prevent me from reaching my destiny.

I DECREE that I will not be defeated because in all these things I am more than a conqueror.

Today's Phenomenal Woman: She's All That!

I am God's girl second to none.
I am God's girl proud of whom He has made me,
my shape, my size neither my possessions define me.
I am God's girl worthy to be loved, and treated
with dignity and respect,
I settle for God's best and nothing less.
I am God's girl who has survived much in life,
my past is my past and my future is bright.
I am God's girl who can do all things through
Christ that strengthens me,
I can reach the unreachable and
conquer the unconquerable with God to guide me.
I am God's girl so strong in the power of His might,
self-criticism, insecurity, envy nor low
self-esteem has no place in my life.
I am God's phenomenal woman that's who I am!

Notes

1. *Cambridge Dictionary Online*, s.v. "Determination," accessed May 5, 2019, https://dictionary.cambridge.org/us/dictionary/english/determination.

2. Greenwood, Becca. "Power of the Tongue: Words Can Bring Death or Life," *Charisma*, February 22, 2015/ Accessed October 12, 2019. https://www.charismamag.com/spirit/spiritual-warfare/22596-power-of-the-tongue-words-can-bring-death-or-life.

3. *Oxford Learners Dictionaries Online*, s.v. "Comfort zone," accessed January 19, 2020, https://www.oxfordlearnersdictionaries.com/us/definition/english/comfort-zone.

4. *Lexico US Dictionary*, s.v., "Decree," accessed November 13, 2019, https://www.lexico.com/en/definition/decree.

5. *Vocabulary.com Dictionary*, s.v., "Value," accessed May 5, 2019, https://www.vocabulary.com/dictionary/value.

Contact Information

To correspond with Dr. Dee, you may write to:
DSB Life Solutions, LLC
P.O. Box 1877
Memphis, TN 38101

email her at:
office@demetriasbanks.com

or log onto her website at:
www.demetriasbanks.com

For information on booking her for a speaking engagement, call: 901-691-5700

or log on to www.demetriasbanks.com

www.ingramcontent.com/pod-product-compliance
Lightning Source LLC
LaVergne TN
LVHW051838080426
835512LV00018B/2944